# Principles of Change

## Teresa of Avila's Carmelite Reform and Insights from Change Management

Kristina R. Olsen, PhD, DBA

En Route Books and Media, LLC
Saint Louis, MO

D0162385

En Route Books and Media, LLC
5705 Rhodes Avenue
St. Louis, MO 63109

Cover credit: Sebastian Mahfood

ISBN-13: 978-1-956715-29-3
Library of Congress Control Number: 2022931785

# Acknowledgments

I would like to express my gratitude to Fr. Marc Foley, O.C.D., Prior of the Our Lady of Mount Carmel Community of Discalced Carmelite Friars in Washington, D.C. Fr. Foley's reading of early drafts of each chapter provided meaningful and helpful guidance. Many thanks are also due to Dr. Sebastian Mahfood, O.P., for his encouragement and support over the years in connection with my teaching of Carmelite spirituality and other subjects at Holy Apostles College and Seminary in Cromwell, CT. I'm also grateful for his editing expertise and guidance and for publishing this book through his company, En Route Books and Media in St. Louis, MO.

# Testimonials

"Countering a view of saints and mystics as detached from the nitty-gritty of life, Dr. Kristina Olsen in *Principles of Change: Teresa of Avila's Carmelite Reform and Insights from Change Management* shows Teresa of Avila very much involved in addressing relational problems and resistance to reform in the Carmelite communities she founded. Spirituality is an interdisciplinary discipline, but Olsen takes spirituality studies in a new direction by drawing from the field of business administration. What emerges is a much richer appreciation of Teresa of Avila's giftedness as Olsen highlights the mystic's talent for organizational management and reform. The resonance between contemporary efforts to motivate people to embrace new technologies and Teresa's approach to inviting her nuns to reform is striking. This innovative work is a significant contribution to Teresian studies."

**– Raymond Studzinski, O.S.B., Ph.D., Director, Doctor of Ministry Program in Spirituality, School of Theology and Religious Studies, The Catholic University of America**

"This is a surprisingly timely book that teaches us how knowledge and religion have existed together for centuries. The book cogently describes how Teresa utilized what we would call 'organizational change tenets' to make major changes in the Carmelite monasteries. Teresa addressed problems not unlike our own today: incompetent management, lax morals, lack of clear direction. Dr. Olsen shows how the strategies that Teresa employed can and are being used to encourage workers to adopt and accept new technology. That includes fostering a favorable attitude toward both technology and change, seeing the benefits of adopting new technology. The author draws on scholarship on 'planned behavior,' managing resistance, innovation, and 'buy-in.' Dr. Olsen knows her topic. For several years, she has taught Carmelite spirituality and other subjects at Holy Apostles College and Seminary in Cromwell, CT. Her Doctor of Business Administration studies culminated in her dissertation on 'The Role of Attitude in the Acceptance and Adoption of Information Technology.' *Principles of Change* shows that leadership, knowledge, and spirituality can be compatible. Indeed, they may be just what society needs today."

**– James P. Gelatt, Ph.D., Professor, Doctor of Business Administration, Univ of MD Global Campus**

# Table of Contents

# Sources and Abbreviations

Unless otherwise indicated, quotations of Teresa's writings, other than her letters, are from *The Collected Works of St. Teresa of Avila*, vols. 1-3, translated by Kieran Kavanaugh and Otilio Rodriguez (1980-87). Quotations of Teresa's letters are from *The Collected Letters of St. Teresa of Avila*, vols. 1 and 2, translated by Kieran Kavanaugh (2001-07).

Section, chapter and paragraph numbers are indicated by reference to the edition above followed by the work within the edition and then by section and/or chapter number and paragraph number.

## Abbreviations of Specific Editions

| | |
|---|---|
| *CWST* | *The Collected Works of St. Teresa of Avila.* Translated by Kieran Kavanaugh, O.C.D., and Otilio Rodriguez, O.C.D. 3 vols. Washington, DC: Institute of Carmelite Studies, 1980-87. |
| *Letters* | *The Collected Letters of Teresa of Avila.* Translated by Kieran Kava- |

| | naugh, O.C.D. 2 vols. Washington, DC: Institute of Carmelite Studies, 2001-07. |
|---|---|

## Works Quoted from CWST

| Const | *The Constitutions* | *CWST*, vol. 3 |
|---|---|---|
| *F* | *The Book of Her Foundations* | *CWST*, vol. 3 |
| *Life* | *The Book of Her Life* | *CWST*, vol. 1 |
| *Visitation* | *On Making the Visitation* | *CWST*, vol. 3 |
| *Way* | *The Way of Perfection* | *CWST*, vol. 2 |

# Examples of References

| | |
|---|---|
| *Life* 11.7 | *The Collected Works of St. Teresa, The Book of Her Life*, Chapter 11, Paragraph 7. |
| *Letters* 172.5 | *The Collected Letters of St. Teresa of Avila*, Letter 172, Paragraph 5. |
| *Const* 8 | *The Collected Works of St. Teresa, The Constitutions*, Article 8. |

# Introduction

For a reform to be successful, it needs to be adopted. People need to embrace it. This was true of the Protestant Reformation, and it was also true of the Catholic Counter-Reformation. Within the Catholic Counter-Reformation, one religious order that was reformed was the Carmelite Order, and it was reformed by St. Teresa of Avila (Teresa of Jesus) in 16th-century Spain.

Fast-forward to the 21st century. Reform in our day often has to do with technology. Both work and recreation involve computers and connectivity. Technology gets "reformed," too, through innovation and new discoveries. We are always updating, upgrading, and upending our old processes in favor of new ones. Here, too, for a reform to be successful, it needs to be adopted. People need to embrace it.

This book draws from research on change management and information technology (IT) adoption to examine Teresa's reform of the Carmelite Order. According to one widely used IT acceptance model (Davis's "Technology Acceptance Model"), in order to adopt a new technology people must first perceive it to be useful to them and easy to use. They must then develop a positive attitude toward it, and finally they will form an intention to use it.[1] Once they have a strong intention to adopt the new technology, it is very likely that they will actually use it.[2]

According to Everett Rogers (*Diffusion of Innovations*), the four elements required for the adoption of new ideas, processes, or technologies are: 1) the innovation itself, 2) communication channels, 3) time, and 4) a social system with established norms.[3] In Teresa's reform, the innovation that needed to be adopted was a return to the primitive Carmelite Rule and a restructuring of Carmelite religious life according to the guidelines established by Teresa and embodied in her *Constitutions*. Teresa's goal was to

---

[1] F. D. Davis, Jr., "*A Technology Acceptance Model for Testing New End-User Information Systems: Theory and Results*" (PhD diss., Sloan School of Management, Massachusetts Institute of Technology, 1986).

[2] I. Ajzen, "The Theory of Planned Behavior," *Organizational Behavior and Human Decision Processes* 50 (1991): 179-211.

[3] Everett M. Rogers, *Diffusion of Innovations*, 5th ed. (New York: Free Press, 2003) 36.

create an environment for contemplative prayer and union with God in alignment with the original charism and spirit of the Carmelite Order. In terms of communication, Teresa spoke to many influential people and wrote hundreds of letters to scholars, priests, benefactors, and others in order to build support for her reform.

The reform took time. Teresa spent the last twenty years of her life traveling and governing the newly established reformed monasteries in seventeen locations throughout Spain. The reform was introduced into the existing Carmelite religious and social system, and to integrate the reform with existing laws and regulations required interactions with governors, city magistrates, and religious authorities. Teresa's reform clearly contained Rogers' four elements of the diffusion of innovations.

The research on how organizations and individuals adopt information technology (IT) is a subset of the more general research on diffusion of innovations and contains specific elements unique to IT. For example, IT adoption research shows that several factors are necessary to bring about the successful adoption of new IT systems and products:

- Intention to use the technology
- Usefulness of the technology
- "Usability" of the technology, how easy it is to use
- Positive attitudes and feelings about the technology
- Social support[4]

Teresa was the first adopter of her own reform. She saw problems in the Carmelite Order in Avila, such as overcrowding, poverty, and lack of focus on the spiritual life. She developed a vision of how Carmelite religious life could be transformed by returning to a primitive version of the Carmelite Rule, emphasizing greater enclosure of the nuns and keeping communities small and manageable. In terms of IT adoption, she perceived that this reformed way of life would be useful to herself and others. She envisioned a way to run the communities that would be simple and easy to follow, although more rigorous spirit-

---

[4] Kristina R. Olsen, "I Think (and Feel), Therefore I Act: The Role of Attitude in the Acceptance and Adoption of Information Technology" (DBA diss., University of Maryland University College, 2019).

ually. And she developed a positive attitude, strong desire, and clear intention to bring about this change. Teresa communicated her vision and intentions to like-minded associates who provided support for her reform.

These aspects of human behavior emerged as a lens through which to view Teresa's reform as a result of my research on information technology (IT) adoption.[1] In recent studies on IT adoption, the cognitive, behavioral, and affective dimensions of human behavior have been examined to shed light on the success of new IT initiatives and their implementations. For example, by examining users' intentions to use a new system, their feelings about it, and how they thought about it, researchers were able to describe how easily and thoroughly a new IT initiative would "take hold" in an organization or a community, with a view toward providing guidelines to influence future rollouts and make them more successful. This could save organizations time and money, improve their reputations, and prevent the need for rework to correct problems.

I made a connection between present-day technology adoption and the "adoption" or reception of Teresa's ideas in her efforts to reform the Carmelite

Order. As in IT, the people affected by the change need to see and understand the value of a new way of doing things, they must believe that it will be useful to them and easy to accomplish, and they should have a sense of excitement and opportunity about the change. It's also important to have social support, and to find ways to overcome resistance to change. All of these factors were present in Teresa's reform.

The book is organized into four chapters:

## Chapter 1: Leadership and Purpose

This chapter describes Teresa's leadership approach and spiritual intentions in light of the civil and ecclesial context of her day. Teresa's strength as a leader was tied to her purpose to establish reformed Carmelite monasteries throughout Spain in the 16<sup>th</sup> century. Her goal was to provide a system of spiritual living that would draw souls closer to God in contemplative prayer and provide for the practical needs of smaller, more manageable communities.

## Chapter 2: Governance and Usefulness

This chapter describes the rules and guidelines Teresa put into place for the reformed Carmelite monasteries. The wisdom and guidance in her details showed how living in a way that was more aligned with the Carmelite Rule and the original intent of the founders of the Order was useful and beneficial for the spiritual growth of its members.

## Chapter 3: Attitudes, Feelings and Resistance

This chapter chronicles some of the opportunities and challenges Teresa encountered in the attitudes of the people involved in her reform. A positive attitude is a key attribute necessary for the acceptance of a new IT system or other major change in an organization. A sense of excitement and mastery can add energy to a new opportunity. However, people with negative attitudes can cause problems and this chapter describes how Teresa dealt with resistance in a particularly challenging situation.

**Chapter 4: Social Support**

This chapter focuses on several key figures who helped Teresa in her reform, including some who are less well-known to readers of Carmelite literature. Teresa had support from Church leaders, civil leaders, members of the Carmelite Order, friends, and family throughout her reform activities. Wealthy benefactors and civil leaders from King Philip II to city magistrates assisted her in establishing newly reformed Carmelite monasteries.

In this book, I focused primarily on Teresa's *Book of Her Foundations*, which described her efforts and adventures to establish 17 new monasteries during the last 20 years of her life (1562 to 1582). This involved work of a practical nature – finding houses, fixing them up and preparing them to be suitable for nuns and friars – and of an administrative nature – establishing governance, staffing the monasteries, and arranging funding.

Interspersed among the stories of the foundations were Teresa's instructions to nuns, friars, priors, and prioresses. Teresa also expressed her personal views on virtues such as obedience and humility, and she related many experiences about her travels and the people she encountered along the way. The *Book of Her Foundations* is a rich tapestry of stories, reflections, and spiritual wisdom.

Teresa put practical elements in place to support the reform juridically, physically, financially, and spiritually. Physically, she made arrangements to rent and buy houses to serve as the first monasteries in her reform, and juridically she obtained permissions from magistrates and city governments to open monasteries in the towns she chose. She also obtained approval from the Catholic Church and the leadership of the Carmelite Order. Financially, Teresa contacted family members and wealthy benefactors who provided funds to buy and furnish the necessary housing. Spiritually, she put guidelines in place to provide for the spiritual growth of her communities and to keep them running smoothly.

Teresa made heroic efforts to create environments where nuns and friars could pray in peace, grow closer to God, and preserve the original mission of the Carmelite Order as it was established on Mt. Carmel in the 13th century.

# Chapter 1

## Leadership and Purpose

Teresa's purpose in reforming Carmelite life was to establish a way of life that would be more consistent with the original intent of the first Carmelites, brothers who banded together on Mt. Carmel in the 13th Century. These brothers reached out to St. Albert, then Patriarch of Jerusalem for the Catholic Church, to request a rule of life to provide guidance and order for their eremitical calling as hermits living together in loyalty to the Blessed Virgin Mary and the Church. Albert wrote what came to be known as the Carmelite Rule, which has guided Carmelite prayer, worship, and community life to the present day.

Teresa aligned her intentions with the will of God as expressed by the Carmelite Rule, the directions of her superiors, and the guidance she received in prayer. She fulfilled her God-given mission with creativity, authority, determination, and enthusiasm. According to Rogers, someone who acts as an agent of change for a new innovation must be able to foster an intent to change in his or her clients, establish relationships with those who will adopt the change, diagnose problems, translate intentions into actions, and put systems into place to stabilize the adoption.[1]

Teresa fostered change using all of these methods. She was very persuasive with people of all social classes, and she had her own strong intention with a clear vision of what was necessary to create the change she wanted to see. She diagnosed and addressed both administrative and interpersonal problems, and she formed strong alliances and heartfelt friendships with benefactors, religious superiors, friends, and the nuns and friars of the Carmelite Order. Through her writings, she put into place rules and governance principles to preserve and stabilize the changes her reform was instituting. Teresa reflected Rogers' characteristics for an agent of change in her reform of the Carmelite Order.

To come to an understanding of Teresa's intentions in following the will of God, obeying her superiors, and providing governance for reformed monasteries, this chapter begins with an overview of the Carmelite Rule which was a guiding beacon for her reform.

---

[1] Rogers, *Diffusion of Innovations*, 400.

## The Carmelite Rule

The early Carmelites on Mt. Carmel were hermits, brothers who lived in community and prayed in solitude. Many were Crusaders from Europe. They came for one reason and stayed for another reason. They became contemplatives, withdrawing from an active mission to adopt a prayerful and solitary lifestyle, among like-minded friends, on a mountain in Israel.

In the early 13th century, this group of spiritual brothers reached out to the Catholic Patriarch of Jerusalem, St. Albert, to request a written rule to guide them in their community organization and daily life. St. Albert wrote the original Carmelite Rule between 1204 and 1214.[2] The first version of the rule was written for the rural setting of Mt. Carmel in present-day Israel. However, after the takeover of the Holy Land by Moslems, the brothers moved back to Europe and settled in urban areas, which required changes to the Rule. The solitariness of an eremitical way of life

---

[2] Kees Waaijman, O.Carm., *The Mystical Space of Carmel: A Commentary on the Carmelite Rule* (Leuven: Peeters Publishers, 1999), 5.

somehow had to be found in the midst of an urban landscape.

In 1247, the Rule was changed by Pope Innocent IV to allow for houses in cities, eating together, praying the Divine Office, and begging for alms.[3] In 1432, Pope Eugene IV "mitigated" this second form of the Rule to allow for walking around outside of the monastery and eating more meat.[4] It was this mitigated Rule that Teresa found problematic, because going outside too much led to dissipation. When she spoke about returning to the "primitive" Rule, she meant the 1247 version revised by Pope Innocent IV.

The Carmelite Rule was written in the form of a letter.[5] It was not only a response to the request by the brothers on Mt. Carmel for a guide to their way of life, but it also sanctioned and validated their intentions and provided reassurance that from the Church's point of view, and in her wisdom, they were on the right track in their approach to spirituality.

The Rule started with a greeting, followed by provisions for the location and organization of

---

[3] Waaijman, *Mystical Space of Carmel,* 11.

[4] Waaijman, *Mystical Space of Carmel,* 12.

[5] Waaijman, *Mystical Space of Carmel,* 5.

communities, the practice of spiritual exercises, prayer in solitude and in community, and working in silence. This was followed by a conclusion and a reminder to remain humble, to serve each other, and to use discernment as a guide.

In Chapters 1-6 of the Rule, St. Albert established basic provisions for the brothers, including the places where monasteries should be established, the choosing of a prior and the distribution of the brothers' cells or rooms. Also included was guidance for eating together in a common dining room and the reading of Scripture.

Chapters 7-13 of the Rule provided instructions for basic spiritual practices. The brothers should stay in their cells and pray, hold everything in common, and celebrate the Eucharist together at Mass. They were to pray the Divine Office, a daily program of specific prayers, in community. If there were some brothers who could not read the prayers in Latin, they could say a number of Our Fathers as their contributions to the prayer life of the community.

Chapter 14 exhorted the brothers to put on the armor of God as described in Scripture, and stay true to the faith. Chapter 15 described the work that the brothers should do, which kept the brothers busy "so that the devil may always find you occupied, lest on account of your idleness he manage to find some opportunity to entering into your souls."[6] St. Paul's life was given as an example, and the brothers were reminded that "those who do not work should not eat" (2 Thess 3:10).

Chapter 16 emphasized silence for the "cultivation of justice," and because "in silence and hope will be your strength." The brothers should avoid talking too much because "where there is much talk sin will not be lacking . . . Let each one, therefore, measure his words and keep a tight rein on his tongue."

The full text of the Carmelite Rule may be found in the Appendix (Pope Innocent IV's text of 1247).

**Poverty, Chastity and Obedience**

When Teresa began her reform in the 16th century, the spiritual practices of the Carmelite monasteries in Spain had fallen into laxity. At the Incarnation monastery in Avila, Carmelite nuns could come and go at will and even invite their friends and

---

[6] Waaijman, *Mystical Space of Carmel,* 5.

servants to live with them inside the monastery. Nuns often went out begging because the community had grown so large that extra donations were needed to buy food. The "dissipation" or lack of a recollected atmosphere was a problem in that the emphasis on prayer and focus on God were hindered. Teresa's goal was to establish new monasteries in which a more rigorous version of the Carmelite Rule would be followed, in order to promote spiritual growth, and in which there would be fewer members in order to keep the community's needs more manageable.

One thing Teresa could do to serve God as a Carmelite nun was to fulfill her vows of poverty, chastity, and obedience (the evangelical counsels). Therefore she "resolved to do the little that was in my power; that is, to follow the evangelical counsels as perfectly as I could and strive that these few persons who live here do the same" (*Way* 1.2). She trusted in "the great goodness of God, who never fails to help anyone who is determined to give up everything for him" (*Way* 1.2).

Not only was poverty a strong motivating principle for Teresa, but also she stressed obedience, for herself as well as for her nuns and friars. Teresa sought guidance through prayer and from priests, scholars, and the teachings of the Church. She also consulted women on how best to proceed with the new foundations, including wealthy benefactors, fellow nuns, and other holy women who had similar aims. Chastity was a virtue that was required but not frequently addressed in Teresa's writings on the foundations. Here we discuss the two most prevalent evangelical counsels for Teresa's work: poverty and obedience.

**Poverty**

Teresa worked hard to make sure her foundations were in suitable places. One question was whether the monastery would be in a large town, where commerce assured it of sufficient income from donations, or whether it could be in a rural area where it would need to be established "with an income," that is, endowed by a single benefactor such that less day-to-day income would be required from its surroundings. To establish a community in poverty caused Teresa much worry: on the one hand, it was in alignment with the emphasis on poverty in the Rule; on the other, it led to many problems. If there were insufficient operating funds, as Teresa knew only too well from her experiences at the Incarnation, life in the monastery could degenerate, to the point that the nuns might return to their homes just to have enough to eat.

Teresa's intention to establish reformed monasteries in poverty began with the first foundation in Avila in 1562. One principle Teresa discovered during her first foundation, St. Joseph's in Avila, was that distraction itself could lead to poverty. While staying with her friend and supporter, Doña Luisa de la Cerda, Teresa had a visit from a holy woman who came to visit her in order to discuss her plans for a foundation. This woman, María de Jesús, also felt called to establish a reformed Carmelite monastery, which she did in Alcalá, a year after St. Joseph's was founded.[7]

The two women discussed the question of poverty. Teresa was concerned that establishing a foundation in poverty, while not a trial for her, could be a source of suffering for others. She was also concerned that "poverty would be the cause of some distraction since I observed certain poor monasteries in which

---

[7] Kieran Kavanaugh, *CWST,* 1: 486.

there wasn't much recollection." However, she "failed to reflect that this lack of recollection was the cause of their being poor and that it was not the practice of poverty that caused their distraction. For distraction won't make monasteries richer; nor does God ever fail anyone who serves Him. In sum, I had weak faith, which was not true of this servant of God [María de Jesús]" (*Life* 35.2). Due to poverty, the nuns felt obliged to go outside the monastery to provide spiritual direction as a way to earn money, or even to beg. This minimized their spiritual "recollection" and contemplative focus on God. However, Teresa realized that with strong faith and dedication to their Carmelite calling, God would provide for their daily needs.

Ultimately, Teresa established St. Joseph's in Avila in poverty, without an endowment from a benefactor and with fewer nuns (no more than thirteen). They were to live a life without the luxuries of the Incarnation, and in dedicated service to the Lord in alignment with the Carmelite Rule. Having realized that lack of recollection wasn't caused by poverty – no amount of begging or earning money could produce recollection – but rather, it was the other way around, Teresa was confident that establishing her first monastery in poverty was the right decision. Recollection, service to God in contemplation, and following the Rule, while limiting the number of nuns in the monastery, would allow God to provide for their needs.

Avila was a large enough city to support St. Joseph's. The citizens were generous and the nuns provided service by praying for their benefactors and talking with visitors at the "turn," a solid, rotating window with a shelf, through which nuns could accept donations. When visitors came to the monastery, they could have discussions with the nuns without the nuns having to go outside the monastery. This helped to promote a more recollected lifestyle.

For rural areas, Teresa eventually came to realize that establishing a foundation with an income would be safer and more desirable. The decision to establish a foundation with an income was first reached for the foundation at Alba, described in Chapter 20 of the *Foundations.* The Duke of Alba and his wife had sent Teresa an urgent request to establish a monastery in their town. She was "not too keen about the idea, because the town was a small one, which would make it necessary for us to have an income." Fr. Domingo Báñez was in Salamanca where Teresa was staying when she received this request. He advised her that the Council of Trent had given permission to establish monasteries with an income, and that "whether or not the monastery had an income or not made little difference in regard to the nuns being poor and very perfect" (*F* 20.1).

Since the Council of Trent had permitted the foundation of monasteries with an income, Teresa would adopt that practice for her future foundations. This allowed her to establish foundations in rural areas, where donations from the townspeople were less prevalent.

**Obedience**

Teresa was intent on fulfilling her vow of obedience to her superiors, to the Church, and to God in her work of the reform. She waited after founding her first reformed monastery until she had guidance from her superiors to establish others. This guidance soon came from the prior general of the Carmelite Order, Juan Bautista Rubeo.

By 1567, Teresa had spent five peaceful years in her first reformed or "discalced" foundation, St. Joseph's in Avila (*F* 1.1). The term "discalced" refers to the fact that nuns and friars go "without shoes," or wear only sandals as a sign of their renunciation of worldly riches. At that time, the prior general of the Carmelites (Rubeo) visited Teresa and not only approved of the contemplative way of life she had established, but also asked her to establish more reformed monasteries (*F* 1.8). The new monasteries, like St. Joseph's, would follow the earlier version of the Carmelite Rule (1247).

Teresa was delighted that Rubeo approved of the reformed way of life Teresa had been living with her nuns at St. Joseph's monastery. Rubeo voluntarily provided "very extensive patent letters, so that more monasteries could be founded, along with censures to prevent any provincial from restraining me" (*F* 2.3). The formal approval by her superior launched Teresa into the final, most active period of her life, from 1567 to her death in 1582, in which she established 16 more monasteries for women and, with John of the Cross, two for men.[8]

---

[8] Kavanaugh, *CWST,* 3:4-5.

In addition to following Rubeo's guidance to establish more reformed monasteries, another way Teresa practiced obedience was by writing down the account of her foundations. In 1562, the same year St. Joseph's was established, Fr. Garcia de Toledo, her Dominican confessor, ordered her to write about the monastery's foundation (*F* Prologue.2). In Salamanca in 1573, Fr. Jerónimo Ripalda, S.J., commanded Teresa to write about the monasteries that had been founded after St. Joseph's. He had seen the account of the first foundation, and he "thought it would be of service to our Lord if I wrote about the other seven monasteries that were founded through the goodness of the Lord, and also about the first monastery of the discalced Fathers (*F* Prologue.2). Fr. Ripalda was Teresa's confessor and also the rector of the Jesuit college in Salamanca.[9]

Teresa gained strength through obedience. She struggled with poor health and she was very busy with "correspondence and with other necessary occupations ordered by my superiors." She felt useless, and that she "wouldn't be able to bear doing this work." However, in prayer, "the Lord said to me:

---

[9] Kavanaugh, *CWST*, 3:414-15.

'Daughter, obedience gives strength.'" This emphasizes how important Teresa's view of obedience was, and how she received confirmation in prayer (*F* Prologue.2).

This wasn't the end of the story. After Fr. Ripalda was no longer Teresa's confessor, she set the work aside because of her many duties and because "I did not want to continue, for Father Ripalda was no longer my confessor, and we lived in different places, and also because of the great hardship and trials." However, the apostolic commissary, Fr. Jeronimo Gracián, ordered her to finish the account of the foundations "little by little as best I could." She complained that she had little opportunity and the task was very tiring, but she continued under obedience: "This I did submitting in everything to what those who know about these things might want to delete. What is poorly expressed, let them delete, for perhaps what seems to me better will sound bad to them" (*F* 27.22).

Teresa submitted her writings to her superiors, and she persevered in the task of writing as a result of the encouragement, support, and direction of those who were her confessors and spiritual guides.

The living out of her Carmelite reform, and her account of the reform, were accomplished within the Order of which she was a part and under the orders of her superiors.

Teresa's emphasis on the Carmelite Rule, and her dedication to the principles and guidelines of the Church, allowed Teresa to develop her reform of the Carmelite Order in obedience to her superiors and for the good of those who would make up her communities. In the rigorous hierarchical context of her day, Teresa established a spiritual way of life that would draw souls closer to God and provide for the community's practical needs as well.

# Chapter 2

## Governance and Usefulness

The Carmelite reform, to be adopted, needed to be helpful to those who entered the monasteries, and relatively easy to embrace. It needed to be useful for their spiritual growth toward union with God, the chief aim of Carmelite spiritual life. It also needed a system of governance that was well-defined and clearly documented.

To provide greater union with God than could be found in the large monasteries of her day, Teresa created smaller communities with fewer distractions and greater solitude. The number of nuns would not exceed 13, but she was open to accepting anyone she saw was truly called to the contemplative Carmelite way of life. The nuns would maintain strict enclosure, not going outside unless absolutely necessary.

In addition to having a building in a good location, practical matters such as water for the monastery were important. One story describes a miraculous discovery of water for the first foundation of friars in Duruelo:

> I don't want to fail to mention the way, considered to be miraculous, in which the Lord gave them water. One day after supper, while the prior, Father Fray Antonio, was talking in the cloister with his friars about the need for water, he rose and took a staff he was holding in his hands and made a sign of the cross on one part of it . . . he pointed with the stick and said: "Now, dig here." After they had dug only a little, so much water came out that it is now even difficult to drain the well so as to clean it. The water is very good for drinking, and all that was needed for the remaining construction work was taken from there, and never, as I say, does the well empty out. (*F* 14.10)

Two examples from Teresa's account in the *Foundations* shed light on her approach to establishing foundations in suitable places with appropriate funding and help from supportive friends. The examples which follow are the foundations of Malagón (1568) and Salamanca (1570).

## Malagón

Malagón's monastery was designed by Teresa herself to provide the best structure and architectural features to make the building useful and beneficial for promoting the Carmelite way of life. At Malagón, Teresa established the initial monastery in 1568, and she returned there in 1579 to supervise construction on a monastery of her own design. This example shows Teresa's creativity in architecture and design, as well as her ability to manage people, including the construction workers.

After all of the discussions about St. Joseph's regarding establishing new foundations in poverty, to accept an endowment at Malagón was a challenge for Teresa. Malagón was a poor place, and it was likely that the alms would not be sufficient to support the monastery. Doña Luisa de la Cerda wanted to provide an endowment, but Teresa was against it at first. However, after she discussed the situation with others she decided to go ahead and establish this foundation with Doña Luisa's help.

Teresa had established two new foundations prior to Malagón - Avila and Medina - and she had spent over 30 years in the religious communities of the Incarnation and St. Joseph's, so she had a good idea what would contribute to the architecture and design of a monastery which would support the kind of Carmelite lifestyle that she envisioned.

The original house in Malagón was too near the busy marketplace, and soon another site was found on which to build the new monastery. The funding would come from Teresa's benefactor and friend, Doña Luisa de la Cerda, who had a large palace in that city.[1] Doña Luisa fully supported Teresa's creativity in this endeavor.[2] The finished Malagón monastery "expresses fully what Teresa thought was suitable for her nuns - the kind of building, the lay-out, the space required," and for that reason its plans are often are used as guides for other Carmelite monasteries today.[3] The granite podium from which Teresa

---

[1] Kavanaugh, *CWST,* 3:27.

[2] Tomás Álvarez, CD, and Fernando Domingo, CD, *Saint Teresa of Avila: A Spiritual Adventure,* tr. Cristopher O'Mahoney (Burgos: Editorial Monte Carmelo, and Washington, DC: ICS Publications, 1981), 30.

[3] Álvarez and Domingo, Saint Teresa of Avila: A Spiritual Adventure, 27, 31-2.

supervised the construction has long been venerated by visitors and local residents alike.[4]

The Malagón foundation was also unique in that Teresa had the nuns provide services for the townspeople "by funding a sewing workshop for girls, and by paying a priest and an assistant to teach boys."[5] Also, it was here that she first admitted lay sisters who "undertook the manual work in the house; they had no choral obligations themselves and greatly facilitated the heavy liturgical commitment of the rest of the community."[6] Elsewhere in her writings Teresa referred to lay sisters with much admiration (*F* 6.9, 11.1, 29.10). A lay sister could sometimes become a choir sister and even a prioress, as was the case with Blessed Anne of St. Bartholomew. Teresa described her as "a companion who has for some time been going about with me. She is a great and

---

[4] Emilio Miranda, *Teresa de Jesus: Vida, fundaciones, escritos,* 2nd ed. (Avila: Asociación Educativa Signum Christi, 1986), 89.

[5] Álvarez and Domingo, Saint Teresa of Avila: A Spiritual Adventure, 32-3.

[6] Álvarez and Domingo, Saint Teresa of Avila: A Spiritual Adventure, 33.

discreet servant of God who can help me more than others who are choir Sisters."[7]

Both the initial foundation at Malagón and Teresa's return there to supervise the construction on the monastery of her own design demonstrated Teresa's creativity, intelligence, leadership, confidence, and management skills, as well as her continuing care for her nuns and the townspeople, and her indefatigable promotion of the reformed Carmelite way of life. Teresa went above and beyond to provide facilities, personnel, and structure in order to make the reform useful to the nuns and friars and to promote their spiritual growth.

**Salamanca**

The Salamanca foundation was established in 1570, eight years after St. Joseph's in Avila. It was Teresa's seventh foundation, and it was requested via letter by Fr. Martín Gutiérrez, S.J., who had met Teresa during her efforts to establish a house in

---

[7] Kieran Kavanaugh, *CWST*, 3:438-9n12.

Toledo.[8] Teresa traveled to Salamanca through Avila from Toledo during the hot summer of 1570. The details of making the new foundation were prepared in Avila, where Julián of Avila procured the necessary licenses and arranged to rent a house occupied by students, who promised to leave the house before November, 1570. Teresa and her five postulants traveled in an open cart from Avila to Salamanca in the final days of October, 1570.

When Teresa and her traveling companions arrived in Salamanca, they found that some students were still living in the house the nuns had rented, and they told the students to leave. They worked hard to get the house ready for the first Mass the next morning. She wrote that since the students "must not have had a gift for cleanliness, the whole house was in such a state that we did no small amount of work that night" (*F* 19.3). With the help of Gutiérrez and two other Jesuits, as well as a carpenter and an official of the city, the house was transformed quickly into a monastery. The new foundation, San José, was formally established on November 1, 1570, at the in-

---

[8] Miranda, Teresa de Jesús: Vida, fundaciones, escritos, 99.

augural Mass celebrated by Padre Gutiérrez.[9] After the first Mass was said, Teresa arranged for more nuns to come from Medina del Campo.

In Salamanca, as in Malagón, Teresa took great care to arrange the living conditions in such a way to promote the spiritual and practical well-being of those who lived there.

## Work, Governance and Administration

Work, management, and administration were important to Teresa as she established her foundations. Her careful descriptions of tasks, roles, and responsibilities provided keys to making her reform useful for everyday activities and keeping the monasteries running smoothly while fostering spiritual union with God.

Teresa wrote many instructions on work, governance, and administration. Her two major documents on these themes are *On Making the Visitation* and *The Constitutions*, which are discussed later in this chapter. Within *The Constitutions,* the sections

---

[9] Miranda, Teresa de Jesús: Vida, fundaciones, escritos, 101.

"On Temporal Matters" contains detailed information about manual labor and selling items produced by the nuns. Roles, responsibilities, and administration are covered in "On the Humble Offices" and "On the Obligations of Each Office."

Teresa also wrote about leadership. She described how prioresses should be sensitive to the capabilities and desires of those they directed. She shared her insights into human nature and described how an organization often took on the characteristics of the person in charge. She also emphasized the importance of the Rule and *Constitutions*, and the role of the prioress in honoring each nun's individual spiritual path (*F* 18.6).

Work had been an important aspect of Carmelite life since the 13th century, when the Carmelite Rule was written. Chapter XV of the Rule states:

Some work has to be done by you, so that the devil may always find you occupied . . . In this matter you have both the teaching and example of the blessed apostle Paul, in whose mouth Christ spoke . . . if you follow him you cannot go astray. Labouring and weary we lived among you, he says, working night and day so as not to be a burden to any of you . . . This way is holy and good: follow it.[10]

Silence and solitude were linked with work and prayer in both the Rule and *The Constitutions*. Chapter VII of the Rule states, "Let each remain in his cell or near it, meditating day and night on the Word of the Lord and keeping vigil in prayer, unless he is occupied with other lawful activities."[11] Teresa's *Constitutions* encouraged silence and solitude by prohibiting sisters from visiting each other's rooms, and by eliminating the common workroom, which could foster too much talking and the formation of cliques (*Const* 8). Working in solitude was in line with the eremitical spirit of the primitive Rule and it would help the nuns develop a sense of detachment from any friendships which might distract them from recollection or serving God, as Teresa wrote in *The Way of Perfection* (*Way* 4.9).

To allow the nuns to maintain their focus on God, Teresa preferred certain types of work over

---

[10] Waaijman, Mystical Space of Carmel, 35-6.

[11] Waaijman, Mystical Space of Carmel, 31.

others. However, the work of the nuns was not their primary means of support – donations were.

The kind of work recommended by Madre Teresa was the peaceful, uncomplicated labor of spinning, without the pressure of deadlines. But women's work, especially, was poorly paid, and a perusal of account books shows that the income derived from the nuns' work amounted to little when compared to the donations.[12]

Teresa encouraged the nuns not to have a deadline associated with their daily work. The nuns should engage in some work, in accordance with the Rule, but it should not be "tarea," or tasks associated with a time limit:

"Work with a time limit [*tarea*] should never be given to the Sisters. Each one should strive to work so that the others might have food to eat. They should take into careful account what the rule ordains (that whoever wants to eat must work) and what St. Paul did. If someone should volunteer to take on a fixed daily amount of

---

[12] Kavanaugh, *CWST,* 3:40.

work, she may do so but ought not be given a penance if she fails to finish it." (*Const* 24)

Teresa addressed the issues of begging and of negotiation about the price for the nuns' work, in the *Constitutions*. She wanted the nuns to live "always on alms and without any income," but there should be no begging: "Rather, they should help themselves with the work of their hands, as St. Paul did; the Lord will provide what they need." If they are "content to live simply," they will have enough, and if they try to please the Lord, "His Majesty will keep them from want." Their earnings should not come from work that requires attention to detail, but from "spinning and sewing or other unrefined labor that does not so occupy the mind as to keep it from the Lord." They should not work with gold or silver, and they should not haggle over "what is offered for their work. They should graciously accept what is given. If they see that the amount offered is insufficient, they should not take on the work" (*Const* 9).

The one thing Teresa did not want was for the nuns to become merchants. Mercantile work, oriented toward production of goods for sale, was clearly prohibited. Neither were monasteries intended to solve the social problem of poverty, at a time when over 50% of the population of European and Spanish cities was poor.[13] In general, revenue from the nuns' work did not exceed five to ten percent of the overall income from Teresa's monasteries. This work was often seen as a spiritual practice to avoid accusations of *ociosidad y pobreza* (idleness and poverty).[14]

The remaining sections of this chapter draw out highlights of Teresa's approach to governance and oversight as described in her two major documents on these themes: *On Making the Visitation* and *The Constitutions*.

## On Making the Visitation

Teresa wrote *On Making the Visitation* while she was in Toledo in 1576.[15] The purpose of this 55-paragraph document was to advise apostolic "visitators"

---

[13] José Antonio Álvarez Vázquez, Trabajos, dineros y negocios: Teresa de Jesús y la economía del siglo XVI (1562-1582) (Madrid: Editorial Trotta, 2000), 284.

[14] Álvarez Vázquez, Trabajos, dineros y negocios, 89,110.

[15] Kieran Kavanaugh, *CWST,* 3:335-36.

in their dealings with nuns and prioresses as they made their rounds of visitation for the oversight of discalced Carmelite monasteries.

*On Making the Visitation* was written 15 years after the foundation of St. Joseph's in Avila (1562), at a time when Teresa had significant leadership experience in managing the new foundations. In it, she advised the visitators how a healthy community should function. Teresa's insight into human nature and her advice on personnel issues reflected her experience with prioresses and nuns, and her emphasis on politeness, respect, and warmth was evident in these guidelines. In one letter, almost as an aside, Teresa made a comment that the writing of *On Making the Visitation* "came as though taught by God. May He be blessed for everything" (*Letters* 116.1). To provide a sense of Teresa's approach to leadership and governance, specific excerpts from *Visitation* are discussed below. These guidelines could be useful to leaders of many types of organizations today.

## Qualities of Visitators

Visitators were to be kind but firm. In general, the visitator should be "affable and loving," however in important matters he should be "strict and by no means lenient" (*Visitation* 3). This firm hand was to strengthen religious observance and to lead toward greater perfection and service of God, not turning aside from this aim "even if the whole world crumbles" (*Visitation* 4). He should not have special friendships with individual nuns. In dealing with problems or strife in a community, the visitator should get multiple perspectives and remain impartial. He should be "holy and prudent" so that he will be "enlightened by His Majesty so as to do the right thing in all and come to know us." This provides good government and allows souls to "grow in perfection for the honor and glory of God" (*Visitation* 45-47, 51-53).

**Frequency of Visits**

Visits to the monasteries were to be regular in order to correct faults and prevent laxity (*Visitation* 5-6). Visitators must not hesitate to remove prioresses who were not well-suited to that position (*Visitation* 7-9). It was more important to establish proper visitation procedures when the foundations were first established because "Greater care is necessary only at the beginning. If the nuns understand that the visitation will be carried out in this way, there will be little trouble in governing them" (*Visitation* 54).

## Financial Matters

Visitators should attend to the financial matters of the houses, carefully examining the financial records and guarding against going into debt. The community should "spend in accordance with their means," even if it meant going without something (*Visitation* 10). Teresa may have recalled the poverty at the Incarnation when she advised visitators not to let the houses fall into poverty. In Teresa's new foundations, this was even more important because all would share everything in common, in accordance with the primitive Rule.

Along the same lines, the visitators should check on the rations of food for the nuns, but "the Lord never fails to provide for these needs as long as the prioress has courage and diligence; experience teaches this" (*Visitation* 11).

Visitators should inquire about how prioresses handle money and gifts. Prioresses should remember they are stewards and reflect carefully on how they spend money. They should be advised "not to be too generous and liberal" in their expenditures (*Visitation* 40).

## Work and Transfers

With regard to work, Teresa stated that the visitators should take note of the work the nuns were doing and thank them for it because "it is very consoling to the nuns when they are at work to know that it will be seen by the visitator" (*Visitation* 12). Work provided a focus for time alone with God when the nuns weren't occupied in prayer or busy with other duties. Teresa preferred the nuns to do simple work, such as spinning, that would leave their minds free for God. Teresa didn't want the nuns to become merchants, although to this day Carmelite nuns sell items they have made.[16]

Visitators should be concerned about the requests of nuns to be transferred. Nuns should not be allowed to transfer at their own request, but only for the good of the Order if they are needed elsewhere. Otherwise, if a nun believed she was being trans-

---

[16] Álvarez Vázquez, Trabajos, dineros y negocios, 284.

ferred because she wanted it, "she will never settle down anywhere, and much harm will be done to the other nuns." The prioress should not show favoritism to any of the nuns in her charge (*Visitation* 18-19).

## Guiding Documents

Visitators were to see that the nuns observed the *Constitutions* and the Rule (*Visitation* 21-22). If they were followed, everything would run smoothly: "I conclude this matter by saying that if the constitutions are observed everything will run smoothly. If there is no great care for their observance or that of the rule, visitations will be of little avail" (*Visitation* 23).

## New Aspirants

Teresa was open to accepting new members, while carefully considering their personal qualities and other factors. Visitators were to attend to the question of whether to accept new aspirants. Since particular friendships could undermine the impartiality of the prioress, Teresa advised visitators to try to see if new nuns were friends of the prioress. New postulants should consider delaying their professions until the visitator made the visitation (*Visitation* 26).

Lay sisters provided important functions in the reformed monasteries. They shared the work and took care of tasks that required interaction with the outside world. In *Visitation,* Teresa advised that lay sisters should be accepted only if there is a need for them and if they could contribute to the work of the house (*Visitation* 27). The personal qualities of new members should be valued more than money or a dowry (*Visitation 44*).

All of these aspects of governance, especially personnel matters, were important for Teresa in order to make the foundations run smoothly. This contributed to their usefulness to the reform by providing written instructions and policies for guidance so that these actions could be repeatable and beneficial to the Carmelite Order. Written instructions also made it easier for new priors and prioresses, as well as nuns, friars, and visitators, to adopt these methods in each community. This promoted the "ease of use" or usability of the reform and enhanced its expansion by making it easier to adopt.

## The Constitutions

While *Visitation* was about leadership and oversight of the monasteries, *Constitutions* governed the daily life of nuns and friars within the monasteries. Teresa wrote *Constitutions* in 1563 for St. Joseph's in Avila while she was the prioress there. They were approved by the Bishop of Avila, Don Alvaro de Mendoza, and later by Pius IV (1565).[17]

*Constitutions* was closely aligned with the Carmelite Rule in its purpose and content. This approach to governance provided the framework to make the reform useful for spiritual growth and easily usable by the community members. It gave nuns, friars, priors, and prioresses a system to follow that would provide consistency across locations and a common ordering of the details in reformed Carmelite life.

*Constitutions* consists of 59 paragraphs devoted to various aspects of living together in community and practicing the primitive Carmelite Rule. In the Kavanaugh translation there are eleven sections:

---

[17] Kavanaugh, *CWST,* 3:86.

1. *On the Order to Be Observed in Spiritual Matters*
2. *The Days for Receiving the Lord*
3. *On Temporal Matters*
4. *On Fasting*
5. *On the Enclosure*
6. *On Accepting Novices*
7. *On the Humble Offices*
8. *On the Sick*
9. *On the Deceased*
10. *On the Obligations of Each Office*
11. *Deo Gratias*

**Prayer**

*Constitutions* opened with instructions on prayer and reciting the hours of the Divine Office in common (*Const* 1-4). Prayer was the most important aspect of the Rule and was the primary purpose and activity in the reformed monasteries. This was aligned with Teresa's writings in *The Way of Perfection* (1566):

"Our primitive rule states that we must pray without ceasing. If we do this with all the care possible – for unceasing prayer is the most important aspect of the rule – the fasts, the disciplines, and the silence the order commands will not be wanting. For you already know that if prayer is to be genuine, it must be helped by these other things; prayer and comfortable living are incompatible." (*Way* 4.2)

The short description of the prayer schedule in *Constitutions* was followed by various activities of daily life, including eating, examination of conscience, receiving Communion, reading, and the practice of silence (*Const* 6-7). Silence was to be observed "with great care," and silence was kept from 8:00 p.m. until after the first prayers of the following day (Prime) (*Const* 7).

**Reading**

Good books should be available to the nuns, and their spare time should be spent in solitude, reading or working, in accordance with the Rule. Reading spiritual books was very important to Teresa, and she recommended specific titles which were to be available in all reformed monasteries, "especially *The Life of Christ* by the Carthusian, the *Flos Sanctorum, The Imitation of Christ, The Oratory of Religious,* and those books written by Fray Luis de Granada and by Father Fray Pedro de Alcántara." Since the nuns' spare time should be spent "in a place where she can be recollected," spiritual reading provided a way to nurture the nuns' spiritual growth and fulfill "what the rule commands: that each one should be alone." Teresa wrote that "this sustenance for the soul is in some way as necessary as is food for the body" (*Const* 8).

The *Life of Christ* was written by Ludolf of Saxony (ca. 1300-1378), a Carthusian monk. It is a compendium of excerpts of works by some of the greatest Catholic scholars on all aspects of the life of Christ. Teresa read this book, and it was one of the two books available to St. Ignatius of Loyola during his recuperation from a cannonball injury in war.[18] The other book Ignatius read was the 13th-century *Golden Legend* on the lives of the saints, by an Italian

---

[18] Kristina R. Olsen, "Work in the Spirituality of Teresa of Avila" (PhD diss., Catholic University of America, 2014), 99-101.

Dominican, Jacopo de Voragine, Archbishop of Genoa.[19] Teresa recommended a different book on the lives of the saints, *Flos Sanctorum,* for her monasteries (*Const* 8).

The *Life of Christ* was written in Latin but was translated into Spanish by the Franciscan friar Ambrosio Montesino in 1502.[20] It was four large volumes, and it consisted of 1320 pages.[21] This book covered the life of Christ in chronological order, containing many references to the Bible and to the writings of patristic and medieval theologians, including Augustine, Ambrose, Aquinas, Bede, Bernard, and

---

[19] Philip Caraman, *Ignatius Loyola: A Biography of the Founder of the Jesuits* (San Francisco: Harper & Row, 1990), 27. Also see William Granger Ryan, "Introduction," in Jacobus de Voragine, *The Golden Legend: Readings on the Saints,* trans. William Granger Ryan, 2 vols. (Princeton: Princeton University Press, 1993), 1:xiii-xviii.

[20] Emilio del Río, S.I., "Introducción," in *La Vida de Cristo* (Madrid: Universidad Pontificia Comillas, 2010), viii.

[21] Tomás Álvarez, *St. Teresa of Avila: 100 Themes on her Life and Work,* trans. Kieran Kavanaugh, O.C.D. (Washington, DC: ICS Publications, 2011), 196.

others.[22] Teresa was reading the *Vita Christi* when she had her famous vision of the place she believed she would have merited in hell:

> "One day on the vigil of Pentecost I went to a secluded spot after Mass where I often prayed, and I began to read about this feast in a volume by the Carthusian. Reading of the signs beginners, proficients, and the perfect must have in order to recognize whether the Holy Spirit is with them, it seemed to me that by the goodness of God and insofar as I could make out He was not failing to be with me . . . I began to consider the place I had merited in hell on account of my sins." *Life* 38.9.[23]

---

[22] Mary Immaculate Bodenstedt, S.N.D., *The Vita Christi of Ludolphus the Carthusian* (Washington, DC: Catholic University of America Press, 1944), 51-52.

[23] Kavanaugh, *CWST,* 1:488n3. Kavanaugh wrote about this experience: "This probably happened May 29, 1563. The secluded spot was one of the hermitages at the monastery of St. Joseph. 'A volume by the Carthusian' refers to the *Life of Christ* written in Latin by the Carthusian, Ludolph of Saxony. The four volumes were translated into Spanish and first printed in 1502 at Alcalá. The medita-

Tomás Álvarez described the *Life of Christ* as having had a powerful influence on Teresa's Christological formation. Ludolph began the *Vita Christi* with a preamble which outlined eight premises that guided the reader "not only for the comprehensive reading of the book but for access to the mystery of Jesus."[24] Álvarez pointed especially to the fourth premise, "An industriousness about contemplating without error the life of Christ," which was extremely important for Teresa's prayer life. Ludolph emphasized picturing oneself at the various scenes in the life of Christ: [25]

> "Be present to these things that were said and done by the Savior as though with your own ears you heard them and with your own eyes saw them . . . examine them as though you thought they were all present to you . . . and read the

---

tion for Pentecost deals with the three stages of the spiritual life: beginners, proficients, and the perfect."

[24] Álvarez, *100 Themes,* 197.

[25] Álvarez, *100 Themes,* 198, quoting Ludolph, *Vita Christi,* Preamble.

things that have already taken place as though they were being done now."

Teresa's recommendations on reading were specific and rooted in her own experience. A common library fostered unity in the intellectual and spiritual development of nuns and friars across multiple locations separated by large distances. The fact that she wrote down what books should be staples in her reformed monasteries contributed to the harmony and stability of the reformed way of live Teresa envisioned for her friars and nuns, and it made new locations easier to set up in alignment with the founder's vision. Such specific directions provided a process that was repeatable in different locations and supported ease of use and adoption of the reform as it expanded.

## Ownership of Goods and Fasting

*Constitutions* next addressed the ownership of goods: there would be no private ownership of anything; rather, everything would be held in common, in support of the spiritual principle of detachment (*Const* 10). Fasting was also discussed, along with the

Carmelite habit and sleeping materials, which are to be coarse and unadorned in the interest of remaining focused on the spiritual life (*Const* 11-13). Teresa emphasized the importance of these matters to avoid the relaxation of the Rule that she had seen occurring in religious houses. Indeed, this was at the core of her reform efforts:

> "These are all matters of proper religious observance. They are mentioned here because with relaxation there comes sometimes a forgetfulness of what pertains to religious life and its obligations. Colored clothing or bedding must never be used, not even something as small as a ribbon" (*Const* 13).

### Enclosure

Questions of enclosure and visitors were handled next. Members of the community were to "pay no attention to the affairs of the world, nor should they speak about them," unless they can offer some remedy, help others find the truth, or console them (*Const* 13). They should avoid speaking with relatives and keep visits short (*Const* 15-20).

## Entering Religious Life

New aspirants should be those who were "healthy, intelligent, and able to recite the Divine Office and assist in choir" (*Const* 21). Nuns who might look to newcomers for the funds they might bring into the monastery should remember their profession of poverty, and that "it is not money that will sustain them but faith, perfection, and trust in God alone" (*Const* 21). The new applicants should spend at least a year in the community to see whether they can "bear up" with the demands of this life, and during this time "they should be treated with complete sisterly charity, and food and clothing should be provided for them just as they are for all" (*Const* 21).

These provisions demonstrated the care Teresa took not to repeat some of the problems she saw at the Incarnation. The problems included admitting too many relatives and servants along with the professed nuns, causing a drain on the resources there, and the unequal treatment of different classes of nuns within its walls. In the monasteries of Teresa's reform, a greater equality would be observed. The decision to accept a new aspirant or to allow the full profession of a nun into the order "should always be done in accordance with the majority opinion of the community" (*Const* 21). In everyday tasks, too, there was an emphasis on equality, as well as an emphasis on the importance of setting a good example. For example, regarding household work, "The Mother Prioress should be the first on the list for sweeping so that she might give good example to all" (*Const* 22). Older nuns and the sick should be cared for graciously, but not pandered to.

**Flexibility**

Mortifications (allowed with permission) and games (not allowed) were discussed next, as were meals (no eating outside of specified times) and conversation (silence may be dispensed with at the Mother Prioress' discretion, ". . . so that all may converse together on whatever topic pleases them most as long as it is not one that is inappropriate for a good religious (*Const* 26). Sisters may talk together later in the evening, and they should bring their work with them (*Const* 28)." Teresa wanted a spirit of joy and friendship in her monasteries, and she encouraged friendly conversation, even at night after Compline (when permitted by the prioress), in order to promote a congenial, family atmosphere in the houses of her reform. This is one area in which Teresa was more flexible than the Rule, which specified the observance of silence "from after compline until prime of the following day."[26]

## Roles and Responsibilities

A variety of roles and responsibilities was addressed in *Constitutions*. These roles included the prioress, the key bearers, the sacristan, the treasurer and elder portress (same person), and the novice mistress (*Const* 30-42). Teresa described each role in detail, specifying responsibilities and the importance of each one's work. Keys were important to Teresa, and there must be three people to open the chest in which the *Constitutions* were kept (*Const* 57). Money was to be placed in the same chest or given to a specific key-bearer if it was a small sum (*Const* 58).

In the reformed communities, there must be financial transparency, and gifts should be received in a spirit of gratefulness: "Each day after supper, or collation, when the Sisters are gathered together, the

---

[26] Waaijman, *Mystical Space of Carmel*, 36.

turnkeeper should announce what was given that day in alms, naming the donors so that all may take care to pray that God will repay them (*Const* 25)."

Teresa's detailed explanation of administrative roles and responsibilities demonstrated sound management principles which could be useful for any organization today. The use of multiple keys held by different people provided the necessary checks and balances to establish accountability for financial matters. She established foundations that would have new entrants mixing with experienced personnel, not unlike present-day corporations. The process of orienting newcomers to the practices of the monastery had to be done while the existing processes continued uninterrupted. Teresa's written documentation of roles, rules, and procedures provided a system of governance for each foundation as well as consistency across multiple locations.

Teresa's composition of the *Constitutions* and *Visitation* closely aligned with the Carmelite Rule provided reformed Carmelite monasteries with three documents which were in harmony with each other and helpful for governing reformed monasteries. Teresa's writing skills were matched by her leadership skills in determining what was most important to write down, while leaving room for what could be interpreted by the individual communities. Kavanaugh pointed out,

> "What stands out in these guidelines for the Teresian life is balance. We find an interweaving of eremitism and cenobitism, of work and contemplation, of liturgical and extra-liturgical prayer. Even the apostolic life is integrated into the contemplative life . . . The practice of asceticism and enclosure are tempered by a family spirit and by gardens and pleasant views."[27]

---

[27] Kavanaugh, *CWST*, 3:314.

# Chapter 3

## Attitudes, Feelings, and Resistance

Teresa and her associates had strong feelings about their efforts to establish reformed Carmelite monasteries. Her activities generated enthusiasm and support among her followers, but it led to strife among those who were against the change. Even among those who traveled with her to found new monasteries there were times of fear and anxiety as they traveled long distances and encountered people in the towns where she wanted to establish new foundations. Often, the townspeople did not want a new religious house in their town, to which they would be expected to contribute alms. Magistrates and city officials, too, were sometimes resistant to the new foundations. Benefactors who expected special treatment, such as the Princess of Eboli in Pastrana, caused practical problems and emotional stress. In this chapter, we explore Teresa's reform efforts in light of the feelings experienced by those who were engaged in it, and we consider how Teresa dealt with her feelings.

The implementation of the Carmelite reform had an impact on many people, from those who were directly affected by the change, such as the nuns and friars who entered the newly formed monasteries, to Church leadership, government leadership, citizens of the towns where the new monasteries were established, and other members of the Carmelite Order. Because Teresa's reform activities affected the thoughts, feelings, and actions of so many people, it may be compared to an information technology "rollout" today.

According to Rogers (*Diffusion of Innovations*), the "innovation-decision" process consists of five steps: 1) knowledge about the new idea and the innovation's existence, 2) persuasion, when the individual forms his or her attitude about the innovation, 3) decision, the choice to adopt the innovation (or not), 4) implementation, when the person puts the innovation to use, and 5) confirmation, seeking reinforcement of the decision.[1]

Throughout the reform, Teresa found people who would listen to her ideas and consider her innovative approach, but she also encountered those who

---

[1] Rogers, *Diffusion of Innovations*, 216.

were against her. Rogers points out that each stage in the "innovation-decision" process can lead to a rejection of the innovation. People may actively reject an idea after carefully considering it, or they may passively reject it by choosing not to consider it in the first place.[2] For example, the governor of Toledo was reluctant to give Teresa a license for a monastery there, but after her persuasive speech to him, "The governor's heart was so moved that before I left he gave me the license" (*F* 15.5).

We see Rogers' five steps throughout Teresa's reform. She persuaded her friends of the benefits of her ideas for the reform, and even before the founding of St. Joseph's, her first monastery in Avila, her sisters in the Incarnation monastery were in favor of her approach. It was from this small group of supporters in the overcrowded Incarnation monastery that the first few nuns were brought to St. Joseph's to form a smaller, more manageable reformed Carmelite community. They knew about the new idea (Rogers' step 1), they were persuaded (step 2), they decided to join Teresa (step 3) and they implemented the innovation by joining Teresa in the new monastery (step 4).

---

[2] Rogers, *Diffusion of Innovations*, 177-8.

Throughout the reform we see Teresa reassuring her sisters and others when doubts would arise, in order to confirm that they had made the right choice (step 5). Teresa's written instructions in the form of her *Constitutions* and other writings also helped to confirm the reform.

In a recent study, the authors described the impact of a person's attitude and feelings on accepting a new change.[3] A positive attitude may help us see change as an opportunity and bring feelings of excitement and a sense of achievement when we master the change. On the other hand, a negative attitude may be associated with perceiving change as a threat and lead to feelings of anger, anxiety, or worry.

Teresa and her associates were often optimistic about the challenges they faced. They saw the reform as an opportunity to serve God more authentically in alignment with the original Carmelite Rule. They overcame obstacles and achieved their goals even when they had little control over the circumstances. At times, however, they felt discouraged and

---

[3] Anne Beaudry and Alain Pinsonneault, "The Other Side of Acceptance: Studying the Direct and Indirect Effects of Emotions on Information Technology Use," *MIS Quarterly* 34, no. 4 (2010): 694.

experienced worry and fear, especially during trips to new cities in order to establish new foundations.

The next few sections provide examples of Teresa's feelings and attitude as she travelled throughout Spain to implement her reform. The reactions of others as she made her way into new cities are also highlighted.

### Avila

In her first foundation (Avila, 1562), Teresa felt much joy and peace: "The five years I spent in St. Joseph's in Avila after its foundation seem to me to have been the most restful of my life, and my soul often misses that calm and quiet" (*F* 1.1). She enjoyed being among her companions. She wrote, "It was a delight for me to be among souls so holy and pure, whose only concern was to serve and praise our Lord" (*F* 1.2).

### Medina

Teresa had many difficulties as she established her second foundation in Medina del Campo (1567). This monastery would be founded in poverty; the

nuns would rely on the donations of the townspeople, and to a limited degree, their own work to
support them. The monastery would be in com-
petition with other monasteries in the town, and the
townspeople resisted this due to the expectation that
they would need to support another religious community. Augustinian friars in Medina also resisted
Teresa's coming. Their men's convent was adjacent
to the house Teresa and her nuns first wanted to rent
when they arrived in Medina, and they threatened to
bring a lawsuit against the owner of that house. As a
result, the landlord withdrew the opportunity and
Teresa and her nuns had to look for another place.

Even though the rented house was no longer
available, Teresa decided to go to Medina and occupy
a different house, which was in need of repairs.
Teresa and her companions arrived in Medina in the
middle of the night in order not to attract attention,
and when they arrived at the house they discovered
it was dilapidated and "in shambles."[4] Teresa and the
nuns worked all night to clean up the house and
arrange a place to have an altar and reserve the

---

[4] Teresa of Avila, *The Book of Her Foundations: A
Study Guide,* ed. Marc Foley, O.C.D. (Washington DC:
ICS Publications, 2012), 48.

Blessed Sacrament. They "worked so quickly that when dawn came the altar was set up, and the little bell placed in a corridor; and immediately Mass was said." With this, Teresa felt she had taken proper possession of the house to serve as their monastery (*F* 3.9).

Teresa and those around her experienced many different emotions while making the foundation in Medina. In her account of the foundation, Teresa reported feelings of anguish and fear, as well as happiness, encouragement, comfort, and calm. She was happy when she saw "one church more where the Blessed Sacrament is preserved." However, it didn't last long because when the morning light dawned, she saw that "all the walls in some places had fallen to the ground and that many days would be required to repair them. Oh, God help me!" She was worried about placing "His Majesty" in the street at a dangerous time and she exclaimed, "[W]hat anguish came to my heart!" (*F* 3.10-3.15).

After eight days in the run-down house, a merchant in Medina offered the nuns the upper floor of his house. It had a "large gilded room" for a church. A lady who lived next door, Doña Elena de Quiroga, helped them arrange for construction of a chapel.

The upper floor of the merchant's house allowed Teresa to calm down because "we were able to keep strict enclosure, and we began to recite the Hours." After two months, the repairs on the original house were completed, and the nuns lived there for several years (*F* 3.14-3.15).

## Malagón, Burgos and Other Locations

In her account of the foundation at Malagón in 1579, Teresa described how happy the nuns were finally to move into their new quarters, "like little lizards that come out into the sun in summer" (*Letters* 316.2). In Burgos, Teresa wrote about the joy that the nuns experienced once they had permission to move into the monastery and resume a cloistered life. She likened it to fish being put back into water after having been taken out of a river with a net: "So it is with souls accustomed to living in the running streams of their Spouse. When taken out of them and caught up in the net of worldly things, they do not truly live until they find themselves back in those waters" (*F* 31.46).

In Caravaca, Teresa experienced joy even in the midst of criticism against her: "I believe that my main joy came from my thinking that since creatures repaid me like this I was pleasing the Creator. For I am convinced that he who looks for joy in earthly things or in words of praise from men is very much mistaken" (*F* 27.21).

Some nuns in Teresa's foundations experienced sadness and the "bodily humor called melancholy," which today we might call depression. Teresa devoted a whole chapter to this concern. She recognized that not all people experienced melancholy to the same degree, but that the nuns who were seriously afflicted could upset the whole community. Teresa advised prioresses to be strict with such persons, and she recommended penance. She recognized various degrees of insanity, and that the faculty of reason could be so suppressed that it led to madness (*F* 7.1-7.2).

Teresa recognized melancholy as an illness, but she did not want the rest of the nuns to start thinking they, too, had this disease, especially if it meant allowing the sufferer to take liberties the others did not enjoy (*F* 7.3). The best approach was to show love in words and deeds, and keep the depressed person busy "so that they do not have the opportunity to be imagining things, for herein lies all their trouble . . . I know that this is the most suitable remedy you can provide" (*F* 7.9).

One example of a person who began with a good attitude toward Teresa and her reform, which changed after her husband died, was the Princess of Eboli. She was a wealthy woman in Pastrana who decided that she wanted to have a reformed Carmelite monastery of nuns in her town. Her given name was Ana de Mendoza.[5] Teresa didn't want to go because she was occupied with her recently established monastery in Toledo. However, she was told that the Princess would take it as an insult if she refused to come, and the Princess had connections with King Philip II of Spain through her husband, Ruy Gómez de Silva. Teresa decided to write to the Princess instead of going in person, but after praying before the Blessed Sacrament, she understood that the Lord wanted her to go, and to bring the Rule and *Constitutions*. Teresa decided to go to the Princess's palace to investigate setting up the foundation in Pastrana (*F* 17.2-17.3).

---

[5] Kavanaugh, *Letters,* 1:623.

Teresa lived in the palace for about two months in the summer of 1569.[6] The Princess caused Teresa much suffering, not least due to reading Teresa's *Life* and making it an object of ridicule in the palace. She later denounced this work to the Inquisition. Eventually, Teresa did establish a monastery for nuns in Pastrana, and one for friars. The monastery for nuns was well-received by the Princess and her husband, and for several years there was peace.

However, after the death of her husband in 1573, the Princess entered the Carmelite monastery in Pastrana as a nun. She moved in with her maids, and she refused to submit to the prioress. She made life so miserable for the existing Carmelite nuns that a decision had to be made, whether to continue to support the Pastrana foundation in the face of an impossible situation, or whether to abandon the project. Teresa decided it would be best for everyone to move her Carmelite nuns from Pastrana to Segovia (*F* 17.17).

The fourteen nuns from Pastrana arrived at the new foundation in Segovia in April, 1574.[7] Teresa

---

[6] Kavanaugh, *Letters*, 1:623.

[7] Kavanaugh, *Letters*, 1:624.

knew when to "cut her losses," although the nuns' departure from Pastrana "left the townspeople very sorry. As for me [Teresa], seeing the nuns in peace left me with the greatest happiness in the world" (*F* 17.17).

Teresa experienced a full range of emotions in the process of establishing her foundations, and she provided leadership, comfort, and advice for others who experienced fear, anxiety, or depression. In the process of overcoming many obstacles, Teresa stayed focused on God and on her mission, which she carried out in obedience to her superiors. The highs and lows of the reform were part of Teresa's life and leadership, and her advice and experiences can be helpful to us today as we take lessons from the account of her foundations.

# Chapter 4

## Social Support

For the reform to be successful, Teresa needed social support. She had an ability to draw people together with a common aim. The support she gained included that of benefactors, townspeople, city magistrates, and the king. Her benefactors were wealthy women who provided houses and property, merchants in the towns to which she traveled, leaders in the Carmelite Order, and bishops of the Church. She had friends who provided spiritual and emotional support, and she found allies who provided financial and practical support. Teresa appreciated the help she received from the people around her, and her accounts of her travels during the foundations revealed her deep love for her colleagues, as well as her frustration with people who caused her problems.

What Teresa did in the 16th century is similar to what the introduction of a new IT system requires today. Any new IT "rollout" requires the support of key allies: top management sponsors who lead the effort, and intermediate managers who orchestrate the adoption of the new system. Change agents – formal or informal – influence participants to consider the new system as a benefit to their jobs and their lives. Sometimes, detractors can derail a project. In the end, the recipients of the change choose whether to use the system or not, but all along the way they are influenced both by the help that they have received from leaders who have promoted the change and by the resistance encountered in the process.

Teresa's supporters and detractors came from all levels of society. The following short descriptions of those who helped her reform provide a few examples of the type of support she encountered. Some examples of those who resisted her are also included. This is not meant to be an exhaustive account of all supporters and detractors. The examples are meant to show how her reform benefited from the social support Teresa received, and how she dealt with various obstacles on the way to success.

## Champions of the Reform

### Allies and Adversaries in Avila

Teresa had much opposition when she first attempted to set up a new foundation, St. Joseph's, in the city of Avila. She renovated her brother-in-law's house and had what she felt were the necessary permissions. The city officials launched a campaign to suppress the foundation because there were already too many religious houses in the city and they were concerned that the new monastery would need donations. However, Teresa found an advocate in Domingo Bañez, who spoke up for the monastery at an important meeting in the city. After her opponents went to the Royal Council to object, other supporters came to her defense.

Teresa suffered considerable inner turmoil as a result of all of these problems. When the opposition to St. Joseph's monastery increased, Teresa was ordered to return from Toledo where she had been staying with her friend, Luisa de la Cerda, to the Incarnation monastery in Avila. She was afflicted by doubts about whether she had done the right thing in founding the monastery because perhaps the nuns who entered there would not be able to thrive in greater austerity. She also wondered about her own ability to live with stricter demands on enclosure and poverty. She was concerned about whether the nuns would have enough food. She went to the Lord in prayer, but "the Lord did not let His poor servant suffer long, for never did He fail to succor me in my tribulations." In prayer, she realized that the devil was trying to frighten her, and she resolved before the Blessed Sacrament to "do all I could to obtain permission to come to live in this house, and to make a promise of enclosure when able to do it in good conscience." This produced a profound change in her: "Once I did this the devil fled instantly and left me calm and happy; and I remained so, and have remained so always" (*Life* 36.9-36.10).

After she found peace, she "journeyed very happily, determined to undergo most willingly everything the Lord desired." When she got to Avila, she found that the patent and brief for St. Joseph's had arrived from Rome. Also, the approval of Bishop Alvaro de Mendoza, the bishop of Avila, had been gained by two of her supporters, Friar Peter of Alcántara, a well-known Franciscan friar, and another gentleman, probably Don Juan Blázquez, at whose house Friar Peter was staying.[1] Teresa wrote, "The two of them succeeded in getting the bishop to accept the monastery under his jurisdiction, which was no small thing since the house was to be poor. But the bishop

---

[1] Kavanaugh, *CWST,* 1:486n3.

was so fond of persons whom he saw determined to serve the Lord that he soon grew fond of showing it his favor" (*Life* 36.1-36.2).

## Domingo Báñez

Domingo Báñez was a Dominican who lived in Avila from 1561 to 1567. During that time, he was the confessor for St. Teresa and the nuns at St. Joseph's. He not only "fearlessly defended Teresa and her work before the irate city council of Avila," but he also gave his approval to Teresa's account of her life in *The Book of Her Life*.[2] At that time, he was official censor for the Inquisition, and one of Teresa's detractors, the Princess of Eboli, had denounced the *Life* to the Inquisition. Báñez defended Teresa's book, but recommended that the work be kept secret. Without the contributions of Báñez, the objections of Avila's city council may have prohibited Teresa's efforts to establish the first reformed Carmelite monastery, and Teresa's reform could have been seriously hindered.

---

[2] Kavanaugh, *Letters*, 1:614-5.

## Friends in High Places

### Rubeo

Juan Bautista Rubeo, as he was known in Spain, was elected general of the Carmelite Order in 1564. He established a program of visitation of Carmelite monasteries in order to reform and correct them. He wanted to "bring the order back to its origins, to stress solitude, affective prayer, devotion to Mary, and the apostolate."[3]

When Rubeo was in Castile in 1567, he met with Teresa when she arranged for him to visit her at St. Joseph's, Teresa's first reformed monastery. It had been in existence for five years, and the nuns there were practicing Teresa's vision for a reformed way of life more closely aligned with the primitive Rule of St. Albert.

Teresa "gave our Father General an account in all truth and openness," and he assured her that she could stay at St. Joseph's. "He rejoiced to see our manner of life, a portrait . . . of the beginnings of our order, and how the primitive rule was being kept in

---

[3] Kavanaugh, *Letters,* 1:659.

all its rigor, for it wasn't being observed in any monastery in the entire order." Rubeo went on to provide patent letters so that more monasteries could be founded, and censures to prevent provincials from restraining her. She had not asked for these permissions, but Rubeo "understood from my way of prayer that my desires to help some soul come closer to God were great" (*F* 2.2-2.4).

Rubeo wrote about Teresa that "[s]he does more good for the order than all the Carmelite friars in Spain together."[4] He was a valuable supporter of Teresa's reform, and as a result of his contributions Teresa was able to establish many reformed monasteries not only of nuns, but also of friars.[5]

**Roque de Huerta**

Roque de Huerta was the chief forest guard for King Philip II. He resided in Madrid. Teresa communicated with him regarding her progress with the reform. He was a close friend of Fr. Jeronimo Gracián, Teresa's long-time collaborator and champion for her reform. Roque helped Teresa by delivering her

---

[4] Kavanaugh, *Letters,* 1:660.

[5] Kavanaugh, *Letters,* 1:660.

letters, especially when they required the utmost secrecy. He was in favor of the reform and kept Teresa informed of the important matters related to the King's governance of the reform. In 1578, Roque sent her a copy of an important order from the Royal Council advising Gracián to continue his visitation of monasteries, contrary to the order Gracián had received from the nuncio, Filippo Sega (*Letters* 256).

Roque was a trustworthy friend, and she called him "brother" (*Letters* 255). She also respected his administrative position. In the very same letter in which she greeted him with the familiar "brother," she addressed the letter to "the very magnificent Señor Roque de Huerta, chief forest guard of his majesty." Teresa's relationship with Roque de Huerta gave her access to King Philip II through one of his most influential advisers, and their collaboration fostered a strong appreciation for Teresa's approach to Carmelite religious life in Roque and his family. His daughter, María, entered the Carmel of Soria in 1581, where Teresa herself gave her the habit.[6]

---

[6] Kavanaugh, *Letters,* 2:606.

# Mediating Family Differences

## Teresa de Layz

Teresa de Layz founded the Carmelite monastery at Alba de Tormes.[7] There was unrest in the monastery, according to Teresa of Avila (Teresa of Jesus), due to some of the nuns' "attachments and childish ways" and issues that were discussed even among friars of another order and among seculars. This disturbed Teresa of Jesus because people would "naturally conclude that all the other nuns are like them" (*Letters* 460).

The niece of Teresa de Layz, Tomasina Bautista, became a Carmelite nun in Medina. Afterward, she went to Salamanca and then to Alba, the monastery which had been founded by her aunt, Teresa de Layz. When Teresa of Jesus appointed Tomasina to the position of prioress of the monastery in Burgos, Teresa de Layz objected, wanting Tomasina to stay near her in Alba. Teresa of Jesus wrote to Teresa de Layz with understanding and compassion, but also with great honesty, explaining that if her niece, Tomasina, did

---

[7] Kavanaugh, *Letters,* 2:609-10

not want to be in Alba with her aunt, she shouldn't be forced to go:

> "She is now experiencing great peace, living in a very nice house, much to her liking. If you truly love her, you will rejoice over this and not want someone to come to be with you who doesn't want to. May God pardon her, for I desire your happiness so much that I wish it were possible for me to give everything you ask for. For love of God do not be afflicted, for there are many nuns in the order who can make up for the absence of Madre Tomasina." (*Letters* 460.1)

Teresa of Jesus had a love of family and an understanding of emotional attachments, as well as the power that influential people could have over her monasteries. She held her own in personnel decisions, and she explained her decisions with clarity and compassion.

# The Power of Persuasion

## Governor of Toledo

Teresa established a reformed Carmelite monastery for nuns in Toledo in 1569.[8] When she arrived there in March, 1569, she had neither a house nor the license to permit her to make the foundation. A number of people had tried to obtain the license for her, including a nobleman who was a canon in the church, Don Pedro Manrique, the son of the governor of Castile. Teresa was discouraged because the reason she had come to Toledo was to make a foundation there, and if she failed it would be publicized. She had not yet found a house, but she was "saddened more over their not giving me the license than by all the rest." She trusted that "once possession of the foundation was established, the Lord would provide as He had in other places" (*F* 15.4-15.5).

Teresa decided to talk to the governor. She began by going to a church near his house, where she asked someone there to go to his house and "beg him to be kind enough to speak with me." She had spent more

---

[8] Kavanaugh, *CWST,* 3:88.

than two months trying to get the license. Teresa was able to get in to see the governor. She told him "that it was hard to accept the fact that there were women who wanted to live with so much austerity, perfection, and withdrawal from the world while those who would bear nothing of this but lived in comfort wanted to hinder these works that were of such service to our Lord" (*F* 15.5).

Teresa used her persuasive skill to convince the governor that the foundation would be an asset to the community and provide service to God. She spoke to him "with a great determination which was given me by the Lord." Her efforts produced success where others had failed: "The governor's heart was so moved that before I left he gave me the license" (*F* 15.5).

This type of support was essential for Teresa to establish her reform. The Lord provided her with a strong spirit of determination, and she spoke persuasively when she needed cooperation from civil authorities. The spirit of determination, combined with articulate speech and reasonable arguments, gained support from those with the necessary authority to help her succeed.

# An Unlikely Ally

## Alonso de Andrada

Alonso de Andrada was a young twenty-two year old student who helped Teresa find a house in Toledo.[9] When after some time, Teresa had difficulty finding a location for her foundation, a Franciscan friar sent Andrada to her to help her. When he first met Teresa, he told her that "that he was certainly ready to do everything he could for me; although only with his personal service could he help us."

Teresa thanked him, and she was "amused . . . to see the kind of help that saintly man had sent us. The clothes this young man had on were not the kind one would wear when going to speak with discalced nuns." Teresa's companions laughed at her and told her not to entrust Andrada with the task of finding a house, but Teresa "didn't want to listen to them. Since he was sent by the servant of God, I trusted that there was something for him to do and that this offer to help had a mystery about it" (*F* 15.6-15.7).

---

[9] Kavanaugh, *CWST*, 3:424n10.

Andrada promised to look for a house, and within two days he had found a house. He had the keys, and he came to Teresa to invite the nuns to go and see it as it was nearby. The house was a nice one, and they ended up staying in it for about a year. Andrada helped them move in and get everything ready for the monastery, including finding workmen. He continued to help them until the work was completed.

When Teresa reflected on this foundation, she was "amazed by the designs of God." For several months "very wealthy persons had made the rounds of Toledo looking for a house for us and were never able to find one, as though there were no houses in the city. And then this youth comes along, not rich but very poor, and the Lord desired that he find one immediately." She appreciated his help and wrote that she didn't think they could have done better themselves in preparing the house and getting workmen (*F* 15.8).

# Recognition of
# the Good Qualities in Others

There were a number of other, more well-known collaborators that Teresa worked with in setting up her foundations. Each provided valuable friendship, a common aim and a willingness to work hard to establish discalced Carmelite monasteries. Teresa's experiences with some of these collaborators are described below.

John of the Cross met Teresa when she was in Medina del Campo. He was a Carmelite friar, but he was considering joining the Carthusians for a more contemplative life. Teresa recognized his good qualities and suggested that he consider joining her reform. He became a major influence in establishing the first reformed monasteries for friars, and he served as chaplain and spiritual director for the nuns. He was the author of many profound spiritual writings, including *The Ascent of Mount Carmel* and *Dark Night of the Soul,* as well as poetry including *The Living Flame of Love.*

Jeronimo Gracián was a priest who joined the Carmelites in Pastrana when he was 27 years old. He became very active in Teresa's reform and led the effort to establish a separate province for the Discalced Carmelites. This was very important because Teresa's ascetical practices, aligned with the primitive Carmelite Rule, were not being followed in the existing monasteries of her day, and to unite the entire order along the lines of the reform was proving to be an impossible task. Gracián was a faithful collaborator and provided much support in the juridical aspects of establishing the reform.

Doña Luisa de la Cerda was a wealthy widow from Toledo who provided a place for Teresa to stay while she was formulating the vision of her reform. She also provided funds for the foundation at Malagón. This was an important step in the reform because up until that time Teresa thought that everything needed to be done in strict poverty. However, her advisors reminded her that the Council of Trent (1545-1563) had approved the type of funding Luisa could provide, and from that time forward Teresa permitted her houses to be established with an income. Luisa was a valued friend and a close collaborator with Teresa, and she provided emotional support as well as financial contributions.

Anne of St. Bartholomew entered the Carmelites at St. Joseph's in Avila in 1570. She traveled alongside

Teresa throughout her journeys to establish foundations. She was Teresa's nurse and secretary for many years, and she was with Teresa in Alba when she died in 1582. She took dictation for Teresa's letters, and she helped Teresa with her many health problems. Anne was a faithful friend and companion throughout some of the most challenging years of Teresa's life and the Carmelite reform.

## Teresa's Social Support

Teresa relied on many collaborators to establish her reform. Without social support, she would not have been able to influence civil and religious authorities to the extent that was needed. She needed help to travel, find places for the nuns to live, improve the houses so that Mass could be said, and arrange living spaces that would foster the contemplative Carmelite life. Also the monasteries had to conform to the Carmelite Rule, which had specific requirements for solitude and enclosure. Teresa found companions who shared her vision, and she relied on God to connect her with people who could help her reform.

Teresa also had detractors, and those who resisted her reform. She demonstrated her under-

standing of human nature and emotions while main-
taining appropriately firm but respectful communi-
cations in her dealings with others. At times, she
needed to distance herself from harmful influences,
and at other times she soothed ruffled feelings and
did what was best for her monasteries. She was a
leader among leaders, and she used her influence
when she spoke to kings and governors as well as
mothers and aunts of the nuns who entered her Carmelite monasteries.

Finally, Teresa worked within the structure of the
Carmelite Order to establish her reform. Obedience
to religious authorities was a powerful motivator for
Teresa. Her attitude toward authority was founded
on her obedience to God, and by acting according to
the will of her superiors she kept the reform on track
within the bounds of her professed faith and her
vows to God and to the Carmelite Order.

# Conclusion

Teresa established her reform of the Carmelite Order one monastery at a time. She developed her ideas about what was needed through observation of what was wrong in the Incarnation monastery in Avila, where she lived, and based on accounts of life in the other monasteries of her day.

With a few loyal colleagues from the Incarnation, she established St. Joseph's in Avila and developed a spiritually more rigorous lifestyle based on an earlier version of the Carmelite Rule. The new approach was more practical due to the small size of the communities and their emphasis on enclosure.

After five years at St. Joseph's, Teresa obtained permission to establish additional monasteries throughout Spain. This launched the reform in earnest, and Teresa encountered both supporters who helped provide financial and other assistance, and detractors who resisted the change.

Teresa needed many of the same elements in her reform that we use in organizational change management today. Her reform required strong leadership and a clear vision, along with a well-defined plan of governance. The content of the reform needed to be useful and beneficial to those impacted by the change. Teresa also needed to develop social support and remain sensitive to the needs and feelings of the members of her communities.

There were ups and downs during Teresa's reform, emotionally, financially, and practically. Teresa was often exhausted, and she needed to keep her spirits up and encourage those around her to do so, too. This is also a factor in organizational change management today because process reengineering can cause major shifts in how people do their work. These changes can be upsetting at times, and they can be exhausting as well. Teresa led her reform with tireless perseverance, and she respected the opinions of those in authority even while challenging some of their assumptions.

Finally, Teresa found many allies in her quest to reform the Carmelite Order. Not only did she have the support and help of St. John of the Cross, Anne of St. Bartholomew and Doña Luisa de la Cerda, but there were also many other less well known collaborators who contributed to her success.

Through her tireless zeal, clear vision, and life of prayer, Teresa led a reform of the Carmelite Order which returned to the original intent of its founders. The separate Carmelite province which was created from her reform – the Order of Discalced Carmelites – embodied the changes that Teresa and her colleagues established in the 16th century. People who enter the Discalced Carmelites today benefit from the focus on contemplative prayer, emphasis on the earlier form of the Carmelite Rule, smaller communities, family atmosphere, and opportunities for solitude. The Discalced Carmelite way of life allows its members to grow toward union with God in harmony with the members of their communities, the Blessed Virgin Mary, and the Carmelite saints who have gone before and worked so hard to provide a path of spiritual growth.

# Bibliography

## Writings by St. Teresa of Avila

*The Collected Works of St. Teresa of Avila.* 3 vols. Translated by Kieran Kavanaugh, O.C.D., and Otilio Rodriguez, O.C.D. Washington, DC: ICS Publications, 1976-85.

*The Collected Letters of St. Teresa of Avila.* 2 vols. Translated by Kieran Kavanaugh, O.C.D. Washington, DC: ICS Publications, 2001-07.

*The Book of Her Foundations: A Study Guide.* Edited by Marc Foley, O.C.D. Washington, DC: ICS Publications, 2012.

## Writings by Other Authors

Ajzen, I. "The Theory of Planned Behavior." *Organizational Behavior and Human Decision Processes* 50 (1991): 179-211. DOI: 10.1016/0749-5978(91)90020-T

Álvarez, Tomás. *St. Teresa of Avila: 100 Themes on her Life and Work.* Translated by Kieran Kavanaugh, O.C.D. Washington, DC: ICS Publications, 2011.

Álvarez Vázquez, José Antonio. *Trabajos, dineros y negocios: Teresa de Jesús y la economía del siglo XVI (1562-1582).* Madrid: Editorial Trotta, 2000.

Beaudry, A., & Pinsonneault, A. "The Other Side of Acceptance: Studying the Direct and Indirect Effects of Emotions On Information Technology Use." *MIS Quarterly* 34, no. 4 (2010): 689. DOI: 10.2307/25750701

Bilinkoff, Jodi. *The Avila of Saint Teresa: Religious Reform in a Sixteenth-Century City.* Ithaca, NY: Cornell University Press, 1989.

Bodenstedt, Mary Immaculate, S.N.D. *The Vita Christi of Ludolphus the Carthusian.* Washington, DC: Catholic University of America Press, 1944.

Caraman, Philip. *Ignatius Loyola: A Biography of the Founder of the Jesuits.* San Francisco: Harper & Row, 1990.

Davis, F.D., Jr. "A Technology Acceptance Model for Testing New End-User Information Systems: Theory and Results." PhD diss., Sloan School of Management, Massachusetts Institute of Technology, 1986.

Davis, F. D. "Perceived Usefulness, Perceived Ease Of Use, And User Acceptance Of Information Technology." *MIS Quarterly* 13, no. 3 (1989): 319. DOI: 10.2307/249008

Dent, E. B., & Goldberg, S. G. "Challenging 'Resistance To Change.'" *Journal of Applied Behavioral Science* 35 (1999): 25-41. DOI: 10.1177/0021886399351003.

Egido, Teofanes. "The Economic Concerns of Madre Teresa." In *Edith Stein Symposium: Teresian Culture,* edited by John Sullivan, 151-72. Washington, DC: ICS Publications, 1987.

_____. "The Historical Setting of Saint Teresa's Life." In *Spiritual Direction,* edited by John Sullivan, 122-82. Washington, DC: ICS Publications, 1980.

González y González, Nicolás. *La Ciudad de las Carmelitas en Tiempos de Doña Teresa de Ahumada.* Avila: Diputación de Avila: Institución Gran Duque de Alba, 2011.

_____. *Historia del Monasterio de la Encarnación de Avila.* Madrid: Editorial de Espiritualidad, 1995.

_____. *The Monastery of the Incarnation in Avila.* Madrid: Alcalá de Henares, 2003.

Kavanaugh, Kieran, O.C.D. "St. Teresa and the Spirituality of Sixteenth-century Spain." In *The Roots of the Modern Christian Tradition,* edited by E. Rozanne Elder. Kalamazoo, MI: Cistercian Publications, 1984.

Miranda, Emilio, O.C.D. *Teresa de Jesus: Vida, fundaciones, escritos.* 2a edicion. *Avila*: Asociacion Educativa Signum Christi, 1986.

Olsen, Kristina R. "I Think (and Feel), Therefore I Act: The Role of Attitude in the Acceptance and Adoption of Information Technology." DBA diss., University of Maryland University College, 2019.

_____. "Work in the Spirituality of Teresa of Avila." PhD diss., Catholic University of America, 2014),

Rogers, Everett M. *Diffusion of Innovations.* 5th ed. New York: Free Press, 2003.

Ryan, William Granger. "Introduction." In Jacobus de Voragine, *The Golden Legend: Readings on the Saints,* translated by William Granger Ryan. 2 vols. Princeton: Princeton University Press, 1993.

Waaijman, Kees, O.Carm. *The Mystical Space of Carmel: A Commentary on the Carmelite Rule.* Leuven: Peeters Publishers, 1999.

# Appendix

## The Carmelite Rule (Text of 1247)[1]

### Salutatio

Albert by the grace of God called to be the Patriarch of the Church of Jerusalem, to his beloved sons
in Christ, B. and the other hermits who are living under obedience to him at the spring on Mount Carmel:
salvation in the Lord and the blessing of the Holy
Spirit.

### Exordium

In many and various ways the holy fathers have
laid down how everyone, whatever their state of life
or whatever kind of religious life he has chosen,
should live in allegiance to Jesus Christ and serve him
faithfully from a pure heart and a good conscience.

---

[1] Waaijman, *Mystical Space of Carmel*, 29-38.

## Chapter I

We establish first of all that you shall have one of you as prior, to be chosen for that office by the unanimous assent of all, or of the greater and wiser part, to whom each of the others shall promise obedience and strive to fulfil his promise by the reality of his deeds, along with chastity and the renunciation of property.

## Chapter II

You may have places in solitary areas, or where you are given a site that is suitable and convenient for the observance of your *religious* life, as the prior and the brothers see fit.

## Chapter III

Next, according to the site of the place where you propose to dwell, each of you shall have a separate cell of his own, to be assigned to him by the disposition of the prior himself, with the assent of the other brothers or the wiser part of them.

**Chapter IV**

However, you shall eat whatever may have been given you in a common refectory, listening together to some reading from Sacred Scripture, where this can be done conveniently.

**Chapter V**

None of the brothers may change the place assigned to him, or exchange it with another., except with the permission of whoever is prior at the time.

**Chapter VI**

The prior's cell shall be near the entrance to the place, so that he may be the first to meet those who come to this place, and so that whatever needs to be done subsequently may all be carried out according to his judgement and disposition.

**Chapter VII**

Let each remain in his cell or near it, meditating day and night on the Word of the Lord and keeping vigil in prayer, unless he is occupied with other lawful activities.

## Chapter VIII

Those who know how to say the canonical hours with the clerics shall say them according to the institution of the Holy Fathers and the approved custom of the Church. Those who do not know their letters shall say twenty-five Our Fathers for the night vigil, except on Sundays and feast days, for the vigils of which we establish that the stated number be doubled, so that the Our Father is said fifty times. The same prayer is to be said seven times for the morning lauds. For the other hours the same prayer is to be said seven times, except for the evening office, for which you shall say it fifteen times.

## Chapter IX

Let none of the brothers say that anything is his property, but let everything be held in common among you; to each one shall be distributed what he needs from the hand of the Prior – that is from the brother he appoints to this task – taking into account the age and needs of each one. You may, moreover have asses or mules as your needs require, and some livestock or poultry for your nourishment.

## Chapter X

An oratory, as far as it can be done conveniently, shall be built in the midst of the cells, where you shall come together every day early in the morning to hear Mass, where this can be done conveniently.

## Chapter XI

On Sundays too, or on other days when necessary, you shall discuss the preservation of order and the salvation of your souls. At this time also the excesses and faults of the brothers, if such should be found in anyone, shall be corrected in the midst of love.

## Chapter XII

You shall observe the fast every day except Sunday from the feast of the Exaltation of the Holy Cross until Easter Sunday, unless sickness or bodily weakness or some other good reason shall make it advisable to break the fast, for necessity knows no law.

**Chapter XIII**

You shall abstain from meat, unless it be taken as a remedy for sickness or weakness. And since you may have to beg more frequently while travelling, outside your own houses you may eat food cooked with meat, so as not to be a burden to your hosts. But meat may even be eaten at sea.

**Chapter XIV**

However, because human life on earth is a trial, and all who wish to live devotedly in Christ must suffer persecution, and moreover since your adversary, the devil, prowls around like a roaring lion seeking whom he may devour, you shall use every care and diligence to put on the armour of God, so that you may be able to withstand the deceits of the enemy. The loins are to girt with the cincture of chastity. Your breast is to be fortified with holy ponderings, for it is written: Holy ponderings will save you. The breastplate of justice is to be put on, that you may love the Lord your God with all your heart and all your soul and all your strength, and your neighbour as yourself. In all things is to be taken up the shield of faith, with which you will be able to quench all the flaming arrows of the wicked one, for without faith it is impossible to please God.

On your head is to be put the helmet of salvation, that you may hope for salvation from the only Saviour who saves his people from their sins. And the sword of the Spirit, which is the word of God, should dwell abundantly in your mouth and in your hearts. And whatever you have to do, let it all be done in the Word of the Lord.

**Chapter XV**

Some work has to be done by you, so that the devil may always find you occupied, lest on account of your idleness he manage to find some opportunity to entering into your souls. In this matter you have both the teaching and example of the blessed apostle Paul, in whose mouth Christ spoke, who was appointed and given by God as preacher and teacher of the nations in faith and truth; if you follow him you

cannot go astray. Labouring and weary we lived
among you, he says, working night and day so as not
to be a burden to any of you; not that we had no right
to do otherwise, but so as to give you ourselves as an
example, that you might imitate us. For when we
were with you we used to tell you, if someone is un-
willing to work, let him not eat. For we have heard
that there are certain people among you going about
restlessly and doing no work. We urge people of this
kind and beseech them in the Lord Jesus Christ to
earn their bread, working in silence. This way is holy
and good: follow it.

**Chapter XVI**

The apostle recommends silence, when he tells us
to work in it. As the prophet also testifies, silence is
the cultivation of justice; and again, in silence and
hope will be your strength. Therefore we direct that
you keep silence from after compline until prime of
the following day.

At other times, however, although you need not
observe silence so strictly, you should nevertheless be
all the more careful to avoid much talking, for as it is
written – and experience teaches no less – where

there is much talk sin will not be lacking; and, he who is careless in speech will come to harm; and elsewhere, he who uses many words injures his soul. And the Lord says in the gospel: for every idle word that people speak they will render account on judgement day. Let each one, therefore, measure his words and keep a tight rein on his tongue, lest he stumble and fall by his talking and his fall be irreparable and prove fatal. With the prophet let him watch his ways lest he sin with his tongue; let him try attentively and carefully to practise the silence in which is the cultivation of justice.

**Petitio**

And you, brother B., and whoever may be appointed prior after you, should always have in mind and observe in practice what the Lord says in the gospel: whoever wishes to be the greatest among you will be your servant, and whoever wishes to be the first will be your slave.

You other brothers, too, hold your prior humbly in honour, thinking not so much of him as of Christ who placed him over you, and who said to the leaders of the churches, who hears you hears me; who rejects you rejects me. In this way you will not come into judgement for contempt, but through obedience will merit the reward of eternal life.

**Conclusio**

We have written these things briefly for you, thus establishing a formula for your way of life, according to which you are to live. If anyone will have spent more, the Lord himself will reward him, when he returns. Use discernment, however, the guide of the virtues.